CAMELLIAS

CAMELLIAS

AN ILLUSTRATED GUIDE TO VARIETIES, CULTIVATION AND CARE, WITH
STEP-BY-STEP INSTRUCTIONS AND OVER 140 STUNNING PHOTOGRAPHS

Andrew Mikolajski

Consultant: Jennifer Trehane
Photography by Peter Anderson

southwater

This edition is published by Southwater
an imprint of Anness Publishing Ltd
108 Great Russell Street, London WC1B 3NA
info@anness.com

www.southwaterbooks.com; www.annesspublishing.com

If you like the images in this book and would like to investigate
using them for publishing, promotions or advertising, please visit
our website www.practicalpictures.com for more information.

A CIP catalogue record for this book is available from the British Library.

Publisher: Joanna Lorenz
Project Editor: Simona Hill
Designer: Michael Morey
Production Controller: Mai-Ling Collyer

PUBLISHER'S NOTE
Although the advice and information in this book are believed to be accurate and true at the time
of going to press, neither the authors nor the publisher can accept any legal responsibility or liability
for any errors or omissions that may have been made nor for any inaccuracies nor for any loss,
harm or injury that comes about from following instructions or advice in this book.

Contents

Introduction

Camellias are the aristocrats of flowering shrubs, producing an abundant display of glorious flowers over a long period from winter to spring. Hailing from the East, they are hugely popular and have captivated gardeners worldwide. With handsome, shiny leaves that are appreciated throughout the year, they make fine specimen plants in beds and borders, in lawns and more informally in woodland. Others can be used as colourful flowering hedges or trained against walls to produce dramatic blocks of flowers. Many are ideal for containers so that they can be enjoyed in even the tiniest of gardens. This book shows you how to grow and care for these beautiful plants and illustrates some of the most outstanding varieties available.

■ RIGHT
Few sights in the garden are more breathtaking than a camellia in full flower.

The history of camellias

Camellias were named by the Swedish botanist Carl Linnaeus (1707–78) in honour of the Moravian Jesuit missionary botanist George Joseph Kamel (1661–1706), who travelled in Asia and described plants found on the island of Luzon in the Philippines. He wrote a history of plants growing there. Ironically, there is no evidence to suggest that Kamel ever actually saw a camellia.

Camellias in the wild

There are over 250 species of camellia mainly found in acid soil in woodland in China. The range extends south to north Indonesia, Java and Sumatra. There are three species in Japan. Around 45 are in cultivation. In the wild, camellias are usually long-lived evergreen shrubs and small trees. Extensive breeding has resulted in over 33,000 cultivated varieties or 'cultivars' of varying size, with a range of flower shapes.

Camellias in garden history

Before being introduced to western Europe in the early 18th century, camellias were long cultivated in China and Japan. Initially they were regarded as tender and were grown in 'stove houses', large heated conservatories which only the very

■ LEFT
C. transnokoensis is a tree-like species from Taiwan, with small white flowers.

them was the English landscape gardener Humphry Repton (1751–1818), who liked to include in his designs areas devoted to plants from specific parts of the world. For the Duke of Bedford, at Woburn Abbey in Bedfordshire, England, he planted *Camellia japonica* (from China, Korea and Japan) with other oriental plants among buildings in the Chinese style. Camellias were also planted by John Templeton of Belfast in the early 19th century, and proved to be well adapted to the climate in northern Ireland, which is warmed by the Gulf stream.

The first recorded camellia in America was a 'single red camellia' imported from England by John Stevens of Hoboken, New Jersey, in the latter few years of the 18th century. In 1800, Michael Floy brought *C. japonica* 'Alba Plena' from England to New York for Stevens. In New York and Boston they were grown under glass, but it was soon discovered that they would flourish outdoors in the milder, more southerly states.

Camellias achieved their height of popularity in the 19th century, when women wore the flowers in their hair or to decorate dresses and hats. However, after about 1870 interest in

rich could afford. It was in such a house at Thorndon Hall in Essex (the home of Lord Petrie) that the first camellia flowered in England, presumed to be a red *C. japonica*. It is illustrated in a picture of a peacock pheasant of 1745. Camellias were also grown in Joseph Paxton's glasshouse at Chatsworth House, Derbyshire, two with white flowers, the other with red. In August 1740 one bore

"a most delightful crimsonish double flower". Other cultivated forms were brought from China by Captain Connor of the British East India Company towards the end of the 18th century, and it was soon realized that they could withstand English winters. Camellias became increasingly popular as garden plants with the vogue for Chinese-style interior decor. Among the first to use

■ LEFT
'Joan Trehane'
is a fine modern
hybrid, raised in
New Zealand
in 1980.

camellias waned, and it was not until the era of the great plant hunters in the early 20th century that interest revived. This was the period when owners of large estates began to plant tracts of land in a naturalistic style. A vogue for rhododendron gardens developed; camellias, which enjoy similar conditions, were often planted alongside the rhododendrons in great drifts, sometimes beneath deciduous trees.

Since the Second World War, camellias have regained their former popularity, and extensive breeding has resulted in a vast range of cultivars suitable for different garden uses.

Plant hunting and camellia breeding

Camellia breeding began in earnest only in the early 20th century. This interest was largely as a result of the finds of two great English plant hunters, E. H. Wilson (1876–1930) and George Forrest (1873–1922). The latter made several expeditions to China, one of which was partly funded by J. C. Williams of Caerhays Castle in Cornwall, England, and by the Royal Botanic Gardens, Edinburgh, Scotland. Forrest sent back seeds of *C. saluenensis* which was crossed with *C. japonica* to produce a range of hardy cultivars generally referred to

as x *williamsii* hybrids. In addition, Wilson sent Williams seeds of *C. cuspidata* (also from China), which has become a parent of several notable hybrids, including 'Cornish Snow'.

Another important camellia for breeding purposes, *C. sasanqua* was introduced from Japan towards the end of the 19th century. While the species is seldom grown, its cultivars are increasing in number and popularity. In the USA it has been crossed with *C. reticulata* to produce a range of scented hybrids. Other species that have been used in the production of garden hybrids are *C. tsaii*, *C. taliensis*, *C. lutchuensis* (the best parent of scented hybrids),

■ BELOW
The enduringly popular 'Debbie'
was raised in New Zealand in 1965.

C. granthamiana from Hong Kong, and *C. fraterna*. So far, however, the dream of producing yellow- and orange-flowered camellias, using the tender yellow *C. nitidissima* (formerly named *C. chrysantha*) from south China and Vietnam as a parent, has proved elusive.

Nearly all camellias grown in gardens today are cultivars deriving from *C. japonica*.

Tea

Camellia sinensis is the source of tea, and since tea is drunk by approximately half of the world's population it is one of the most important

■ BELOW
C. sinensis is the tea plant. Only the fresh young tips are picked and used.

economic plants. In the wild, it can achieve tree-like proportions, attaining a height of some 6m (20ft), but in cultivation it is kept to a low, rounded shrub, with frequent pruning encouraging fresh, soft growth for harvesting.

There are two main varieties of tea plant, the small-leaved China tea (*C. sinensis sinensis*) and the large-leaved Assam plant (*C. sinensis* 'Assamica'). Hybrids between the two are also grown. Most tea is produced from the Assam plant.

Camellias in the garden

Camellias have a variety of uses in gardens of every size, whether a large country plot or a small courtyard. They are effective planted in isolation as eye-catching specimens or combined with other plants in shrub or mixed borders. Some can be grown as hedges, while many make suitable wall shrubs, and a few can be formally wall-trained (see Cultivation; Pruning

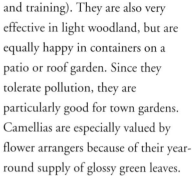

and training). They are also very effective in light woodland, but are equally happy in containers on a patio or roof garden. Since they tolerate pollution, they are particularly good for town gardens. Camellias are especially valued by flower arrangers because of their year-round supply of glossy green leaves.

Camellias flower from late autumn to early summer. Cultivars of *C. japonica* and *C.* x *williamsii* are the most popular, their season extending from late winter to late spring. The cultivars of *C. sasanqua*, some with scented flowers, flower in autumn and winter. Cultivars of *C. reticulata* flower in spring, but they are seldom grown, despite being among the most spectacular of all camellias. They are not reliably hardy in cold districts and in time become very large plants, suitable only for big sheltered gardens or large conservatories. Moreover, they are difficult to propagate and are available only from specialist nurseries (see Buying).

Camellias have an undeserved reputation for being difficult to grow. Given the right conditions (see Cultivation), they are sturdy shrubs that grow vigorously and will flower freely.

■ RIGHT
Most camellias
thrive in light
woodland.

■ OPPOSITE
Camellias combine
well with other
acid-loving
plants, such as
rhododendrons.

Specimens

Camellias make wonderful specimens
provided you choose a variety that is
reliably hardy in your area. With their
lustrous, healthy foliage, they are
handsome plants even when not in
flower. Sturdy, upright cultivars that
flower freely are ideal. 'Donation',
'Leonard Messel' and 'Debbie' are all
outstanding pinks. The American-
bred 'Spring Festival' is charming
when its dainty pink flowers appear
among the bronze-tinged young
leaves, but it needs a fairly sheltered
position. White cultivars are generally
less suitable, since the flowers are
more susceptible to frost damage,
but 'Commander Mulroy' and

'Janet Waterhouse' are well worth
trying. For a good red, try 'Bob
Hope'. To keep specimens compact
and bushy, trim them after flowering
(see Pruning and training).

Growing against walls

Many camellias benefit from the
shelter and protection of a wall or
fence, especially early-flowering
varieties that are susceptible to frost
damage. Camellias with flexible stems
can be formally trained to produce a
flat block of flowers making one of
the most impressive sights in the
garden. Exploit a warm wall by
planting a variety against it which
would not otherwise be hardy, such

as 'Snowflake', which bears single
white flowers in the depths of winter.
The heat of the wall will provide
adequate protection against the
ravages of winter. There are many
more camellias that thrive in the
cooler conditions provided by a
partially shaded wall, which will
provide a microclimate similar to
that provided by a woodland setting.

Plant companions

In a large garden, camellias are
effective when planted in groups,
either mixed or of one variety.
They can also be planted with other
flowering shrubs to provide year-
round interest or a dramatic seasonal

■ BELOW

A camellia planted with *Viburnum tinus* and *Elaeagnus* makes an effective backdrop to spring-flowering perennials.

display. Early-flowering shrubs that make suitable companions include witch hazel (*Hamamelis*), magnolias, rhododendrons and *Pieris* (some of which also require acid soil). White camellias team well with white or wine-purple magnolias, while pinks stand out against purple- or mauve-flowering rhododendrons such as 'Blue Diamond' or 'Purple Splendour'. Red camellias need

careful placing: for a dazzling effect, plant them among the vivid red foliage of *Pieris* 'Forest Flame'.

If you prefer to let your camellias make their own statement without competition when in flower, plant them with other evergreens, such as eucryphias, which flower in late summer and do not vie for your attention, *Viburnum tinus* or the spotted laurel, *Aucuba japonica*

'Crotonifolia'. *Choisya ternata* and *Elaeagnus* offer other possibilities. Or combine early-flowering camellias such as 'Cornish Snow' with Christmas box (*Sarcococca humilis*).

In a mixed planting, spring bulbs such as anemones, daffodils (*Narcissus*) and species tulips make ideal companions, as do the blue chionodoxas, scillas and bluebells (*Hyacinthoides*). As for herbaceous

■ RIGHT
'Lavinia Maggi'
is a striking
cultivar with
striped flowers.

perennials, bergenias have
comparably glossy leaves, and the
white, pink or beetroot-red flowers
blend well with the camellias.
Other suitable perennials include
Dicentra, the beautiful Himalayan
blue poppy (*Meconopsis betonicifolia*),
Solomon's seal (*Polygonatum* x
hybridum) and foxgloves (*Digitalis*),
as well as blue-flowered *Omphalodes
cappadocica* and primulas. For interest
later in the season, follow these with
shade-loving hostas, periwinkle
(*Vinca*) or London pride (*Saxifraga* x
urbium). For a Japanese look, site
your camellias among Japanese
maples (*Acer japonicum* and
A. palmatum) and underplant
with hostas and ferns.

If you have a woodland or
sheltered, shady part of the garden,

■ BELOW
'Cornish Spring' is a hybrid with
dainty flowers that combine well
with shade-loving primulas.

pink camellias such as 'Donation'
or 'Brigadoon' can be grown with
camassias, either the white
C. leichtlinii or blue *C. cusickii*.
A carpet of *Anemone blanda* is also
highly effective. For a gentle scheme,
underplant a pale pink or white
camellia with drifts of 'White
Splendour' and richer pinks with the
deep pink 'Charmer'. For a stronger
look, team a red camellia such
as 'Grand Prix' with the blue
'Atrocaerulea' or magenta 'Radar'.

In summer, in a fairly open site,
camellias can become backdrops to
vivid annuals or summer bulbs, such
as lilies and white *Galtonia candicans*.
For interest later in the season, in a
reasonably damp climate, a strong,
vigorous upright camellia can be an
excellent host to the sensational

Flame creeper *Tropaeolum speciosum*, a herbaceous climber with brilliant crimson flowers that stand out among the glossy camellia leaves. Alternatively, use a vigorous camellia as an informal support for a lax gallica rose such as 'Belle de Crécy', which likes nothing better than to wrap its branches around an accommodating neighbour.

Camellia hedges

Camellias can make the most stylish of evergreen hedges, provided you choose hardy varieties. They are not, however, suitable as windbreaks. Slow-growing varieties with a compact habit are best, since they need minimum pruning to keep them

CAMELLIAS SUITABLE FOR HEDGING

| 'Anticipation' |
| 'Charles Colbert' |
| 'Commander Mulroy' |
| 'Debbie' |
| 'Forest Green' |
| 'Free Style' |
| 'Jury's Yellow' |
| 'Just Darling' (does not flower freely in the UK) |
| 'Laura Boscawen' |
| 'Margaret Waterhouse' |
| 'Matterhorn' |
| 'Roger Hall' (does not flower freely in the UK) |
| 'Señorita' |
| 'Spring Festival' |
| 'Tiptoe' |

tight (see Pruning and training). Among the most suitable are 'Tiptoe' (pink), 'Jury's Yellow' (white with pale yellow centres) and 'Señorita' (rose pink). It is best to restrict yourself to one variety. A mixed hedge is an attractive idea, but different varieties have different habits and flowering times, and they are unlikely to merge to form a solid mass of foliage.

Camellias in containers

Camellias make excellent specimen plants in large containers. Oriental-style pots are particularly sympathetic, reflecting the eastern origins of the plants. Provided they are not too heavy, camellias in

■ BELOW
Upright-growing camellias make
good specimens.

containers can be moved around the garden at will. Stand them near the house, where they can be enjoyed from a window. Alternatively, use them to mark a focal point, provided the site is not exposed, or use them in pairs of the same variety to flank a door. In summer, when out of flower, they make splendid companions to other shade-loving plants such as hostas and ferns. Such a combination provides a restful mix at the height of summer, a symphony of green when your borders are alight with more dramatic colours.

Camellias under glass

In cold districts, winter-flowering camellias that are of borderline hardiness make excellent subjects for growing in a cool greenhouse or unheated conservatory. This is also the best way of producing perfect flowers on camellias such as 'Janet Waterhouse' that are prone to frost damage. Unless you have a very large space, choose a smaller, compact variety such as 'Mignonne' (pale pink) or 'Yuletide' (red). Other plants that thrive in containers and enjoy the same conditions include *Dicentra* and cool-growing orchids such as *Cymbidium*.

Botany and flower shapes

Semi-double flower

Camellias are evergreen shrubs and small trees. Most are hardy down to -10°C (14°F), but a few are tropical plants that cannot survive frost. Their leaves, carried alternately on the stems, are usually glossy and have toothed margins. Most species produce flowers that are white, pink or red, but a few sub-tropical species, such as *C. nitidissima*, have yellow flowers. The flowers can be produced singly, or in pairs or clusters.

Extensive breeding has resulted in plants with a range of flower shapes: single, semi-double, anemone-form, peony-form, rose-form double and formal double. Classification by flower shape is not hard and fast.

'Bob Hope' can produce flowers which are both semi-double and peony-form on the same bush. 'Rose Parade' can be classified as a rose-form or formal double. Furthermore, shape and size can be affected by the climate and season: flowers tend to be bigger in warmer climates. Flowering times can vary from year to year, depending on the severity of the winter and the warmth of the spring.

Definitions of flower shapes

• **Single flowers** have one row of not more than eight petals with a central group of conspicuous stamens (the male part of the flower, borne at the ends of filaments). They are usually saucer-shaped, but can also be cup or trumpet-shaped.

• **Semi-double flowers** have two or more rows of petals with a central group of conspicuous stamens.

• **Anemone-form flowers** have one or more rows of large, outer petals and a central mass of petaloids (modified stamens that are petal-like).

• **Peony-form flowers** have an irregular arrangement of petals, petaloids and stamens. They are deep and rounded in shape.

Rose-form double flower

Single flower

Anemone-form flower

Peony-
form flower

• **Rose-form double flowers** have formally arranged petals that taper to a point and overlap slightly. When fully open, the centre is concave and the stamens are visible.

• **Formal double flowers** have many rows of petals, formally arranged, with no stamens visible.

Most of the camellias grown in gardens today can be defined as cultivars of *C. japonica*, *C.* x *williamsii*, *C. sasanqua* or *C. reticulata*. A few are hybrids with other species such as *C. cuspidata* or are of more complex parentage (e.g. 'Cornish Snow' and 'Leonard Messel') and are usually grouped as 'hybrids'. There is also a group of camellias referred to as 'Higo japonicas'. These were cultivated in the city of Higo (now Kumamoto) in Japan, and characteristically have single flowers with large bosses of golden-yellow stamens. In this book, all hybrid camellias are referred to by their cultivar name only.

EXAMPLES OF FLOWER SHAPES

• SINGLE
'Cornish Snow', 'Cornish Spring', 'Jupiter', 'St Ewe'

• SEMI-DOUBLE
'Adolphe Audusson', 'Akashigata', 'Berenice Boddy', 'Bowen Bryant', 'Brigadoon', 'Daintiness', 'Dr Tinsley', 'Donation', 'Gloire de Nantes', 'Grand Prix', 'Grand Slam', 'Inspiration', 'Leonard Messel', 'Muskoka'

• ANEMONE-FORM
'Bob's Tinsie', 'Jury's Yellow'

• PEONY-FORM
'Anticipation', 'Bob Hope', 'Debbie', 'Hakurakuten'

• ROSE-FORM DOUBLE
'Joan Trehane', 'Rose Parade'

• FORMAL DOUBLE
'C. M. Hovey', 'Galaxie', 'Konronkoku', 'Nuccio's Gem', 'Spring Festival', 'Water Lily'

Formal double flower

Species camellias

Plant Directory

In the following directory, camellias are divided into species (listed alphabetically) and hybrids (sorted by colour: white, pink, bicolours, red).

The heights and spreads cited are those the plant can be expected to achieve given ideal growing conditions. They may vary, depending on the soil type and climate. Some are slow-growing and may take many years to reach full size; others can exceed the dimensions given here. The size of all camellias can be controlled by pruning (see Pruning and training).

Flower colour and shape can also vary, depending on the season and climate.

Unless indicated otherwise, all the camellias described here are hardy to -10°C (14°F).

■ ABOVE

C. FRATERNA

Species camellia from China. In late winter to early spring, small, fragrant white flowers (sometimes tinted lilac) appear. The elliptic, glossy dark green leaves have black-tipped teeth. Height and spread in the wild to 5m (16½ft). In cold climates, *C. fraterna* should be grown in a container under glass.

■ RIGHT

C. CUSPIDATA

Species camellia from southern China, where it is widely distributed. Small, single white flowers appear on an upright, slender shrub from late winter to mid-spring. The leaves are lance-shaped to broadly elliptic and are glossy dark green. Height and spread in the wild to 3m (10ft). Not reliably hardy, *C. cuspidata* is best grown in a container and over-wintered under glass in cold districts.

■ RIGHT AND INSET
C. LUTCHUENSIS

Species camellia from the Liu Kiu islands
of southern Japan and from Taiwan. Small,
very fragrant, single white flowers appear in
late winter. The small, pointed, elliptic to
oblong leaves are bright red when young.
Height and spread in the wild to 3m (10ft).
C. lutchuensis can be grown outdoors only
in frost-free climates; it makes a spreading,
rounded tree or shrub.

 RIGHT
C. TSAII

Species camellia from southern China,
Burma and northern Vietnam. In mid-
and late winter, tiny white flowers hang
from the branches. The glossy dark
green leaves, which may be shed during
prolonged cold spells, have wavy margins.
Height and spread in the wild to 5m
(16½ft). *C. tsaii* does not withstand frost;
in cold climates, grow it in a container
and overwinter it under glass.

Hybrid camellias

■ BELOW

'E. T. R. CARLYON'

Cultivar of *C.* x *williamsii* hybrid, introduced in 1972.
In mid- and late spring, long, arching branches are wreathed
with medium-sized, semi-double to rose-form white flowers.
Height 2.5m (8ft), spread 2m (6½ft). 'E. T. R. Carlyon' is
among the most reliable of the white camellias.

■ ABOVE

'CORNISH SNOW'

Hybrid camellia (*C. cuspidata* x *C. saluenensis*), introduced in 1950.
Small, dainty, single white flowers, produced in abundance, open
from pink-tinted buds from mid-winter to late spring. The leaves
are bronze on emergence, maturing to dark green. Height 3m
(10ft), spread 1.5m (5ft). Owing to its early flowering season,
'Cornish Snow' is best in a sheltered spot in cold climate areas.

■ BELOW

'JANET WATERHOUSE'

Cultivar of *C. japonica*, introduced in 1952. From mid- to late spring, it produces medium-sized, white flowers that vary in form depending on the climate. In warm areas they are semi-double, in colder areas formal double. Height and spread 3m (10ft). 'Janet Waterhouse' is a sturdy, upright camellia.

■ ABOVE RIGHT

'JURY'S YELLOW'

Cultivar of *C. x williamsii*, introduced in 1976. From mid- to late spring it carries an abundance of medium-sized, anemone-form to peony-form flowers. The outer petals are creamy-white and wavy-edged; the central petaloids are creamy-yellow. Height 2.5m (8ft), spread 2m (6½ft). Forming a dense, cone-shaped bush, 'Jury's Yellow' is the closest to a yellow camellia; it has a long flowering season.

■ RIGHT

'NUCCIO'S JEWEL'

Cultivar of *C. japonica*, introduced in 1978. From mid- to late spring it produces medium-sized, peony-form, white flowers that are flushed with pale pink. Height and spread 3m (10ft). Slow-growing, 'Nuccio's Jewel' is a good choice for a container.

■ ABOVE
'BERENICE BODDY'

Cultivar of *C. japonica*, introduced in
1946. Large, semi-double pale pink flowers
(with deeper pink lower petals) appear
from late winter to late spring. Height and
spread 3m (10ft). An exceptionally hardy
cultivar that is wind tolerant, 'Berenice
Boddy' is a vigorous, quick-growing
spreading shrub.

■ LEFT
'DR TINSLEY'

Cultivar of *C. japonica*, introduced
in 1949. Medium-sized, semi-double
(sometimes loose peony-form or formal
double) flowers have petals that are very
pale pink at the base, becoming deeper
pink towards the edges. The leaves are
glossy dark green. Height and spread 3m
(10ft). 'Dr Tinsley' is a compact, upright
camellia that tolerates windy sites.

■ ABOVE

'AVE MARIA'

Cultivar of *C. japonica*, introduced in 1956. Small to medium-sized formal double, pale pink flowers, darker at the centre, appear from early to late spring. Height and spread 3m (10ft). 'Ave Maria' is slow growing, bushy and compact; it thrives in a container.

■ LEFT

'J. C. WILLIAMS'

Cultivar of *C.* x *williamsii*, introduced in 1940. In mid- to late spring, arching branches carry a profusion of medium-sized, single, pale blush-pink flowers with broad, wavy petals. Height and spread to 5m (16½ft). 'J. C. Williams', named in honour of the great camellia grower, has fan-shaped branches that make it suitable for wall-training.

■ ABOVE
'LASCA BEAUTY'

Hybrid camellia (*C. reticulata* x
C. japonica), introduced in 1974.
Very large, semi-double, soft pink flowers
with thick petals emerge in mid-spring.
The elliptic leaves are dark green.
Height to 5m (16½ft), spread to 3m
(10ft). 'Lasca Beauty' is one of the most
sumptuous of all camellias.

■ LEFT
'BRIGADOON'

Cultivar of *C.* x *williamsii*, introduced in
1960. Large, very double, soft silvery pink
flowers with yellow stamens appear in
mid- and late spring. The leaves are bright
glossy green. Height 2.5m (8ft), spread
2m (6½ft). One of the most popular of
all camellias, 'Brigadoon' is dense and
upright; it is exceptionally hardy.

■ BELOW

'DONATION'

Cultivar of *C. x williamsii*, introduced in 1941. From late winter to late spring, a profusion of large, semi-double pink flowers, veined darker pink, with yellow stamens, appear amid bright, glossy green foliage. Height 5m (16½ft), spread 2.5m (8ft). 'Donation' is popular because of its vigour and profusion of flowering.

■ ABOVE

'SPRING FESTIVAL'

Hybrid camellia (a seedling of *C. cuspidata*), introduced in 1975. In mid- to late spring, it carries small, dainty, formal double, light pink flowers among small, elliptic, dark green leaves that are tinged bronze when young. Height to 4m (13ft), spread to 2m (6½ft). With its narrow, upright habit, 'Spring Festival' makes an excellent specimen in a sheltered garden or as a container plant.

■ LEFT

'CONTRIBUTION'

Cultivar of *C. x williamsii* introduced in 1996. From mid- to late spring, it produces masses of semi-double, rose-pink flowers. Height 1m (3ft), spread 1.5m (5ft). Horizontal and spreading, 'Contribution' is ideal for small gardens; it enjoys a shady site.

■ ABOVE

'LADY LOCH'

Cultivar of *C. japonica*, introduced in 1898. In spring, it produces medium-sized, peony-form flowers with pink petals that become white at the edges and are sometimes veined darker pink. The glossy dark green leaves curve downwards. Height 3m (10ft), spread 2m (6½ft). Dense and upright, 'Lady Loch' is long-flowering.

■ ABOVE

'LEONARD MESSEL'

Hybrid camellia (*C. x williamsii* 'Mary Christian' x *C. reticulata*), introduced in 1958. In early to late spring, it carries a profusion of large, semi-double to peony-form, deep pink flowers that are veined with darker pink. The oval leaves are matt dark green. Height 4m (13ft), spread 3m (10ft). 'Leonard Messel' is exceptionally hardy and vigorous, and has a long flowering season.

■ RIGHT
'JOAN
TREHANE'

Cultivar of
C. x *williamsii*,
introduced in
1980. From mid-
to late spring, it
produces large,
rose-form double,
clear pink flowers.
Height 2.5m (8ft),
spread 2m (6½ft).
'Joan Trehane' is
strong, upright
and vigorous.

■ RIGHT
'MARY LARCOM'

Cultivar of *C.* x *williamsii*. In mid- to late
spring, it carries an abundance of single,
soft pink flowers with golden stamens
among blunt-tipped leaves. Height and
spread to 4m (13ft). 'Mary Larcom' is
a large, rounded and open shrub.

■ ABOVE

'INSPIRATION'

Hybrid camellia (*C. reticulata* x
C. saluenensis), introduced in 1954.
From mid-winter to late spring,
medium-sized, semi-double deep pink
flowers appear among oval, glossy deep
green leaves. Height 4m (13ft), spread
2m (6½ft). 'Inspiration' makes a fine
specimen or wall shrub where space
permits; it is one of the hardiest and
most reliable offspring of *C. reticulata*.

■ RIGHT

'TOMORROW'S DAWN'

Cultivar of *C. japonica*. Medium-sized,
semi-double warm pink flowers open to
reveal yellow stamens in spring. Height
and spread 3m (10ft). 'Tomorrow's
Dawn' is an elegant, open shrub.

■ LEFT

'MUSKOKA'

Cultivar of *C.* x *williamsii*, introduced in 1979. From early to late spring, it carries medium-sized, semi-double pink flowers that are veined with darker pink. Height 2.5m (8ft), spread 2m (6½ft). 'Muskoka' is a good choice for a container.

■ ABOVE

'DEBBIE'

Cultivar of *C.* x *williamsii*, introduced in 1965. From late winter to late spring, medium-sized, peony-form, clear deep pink flowers appear among glossy bright green leaves. Height to 3m (10ft), spread to 2m (6½ft). Upright and vigorous, 'Debbie' is valued for its long season and prolific flowering.

■ ABOVE

'GOLDEN SPANGLES'

Cultivar of *C.* x *williamsii*, introduced in 1960. Funnel-shaped, single, pinkish-red flowers, with yellow stamens, appear in mid- to late spring among leaves that are splashed centrally with yellow-green. Height 2.5m (8ft), spread 2m (6½ft). A sport of 'Mary Christian', 'Golden Spangles' is almost unique among camellias because it is grown for its foliage instead of its flowers.

■ LEFT
'ST EWE'

Cultivar of *C.* x *williamsii*, introduced in 1947. In early to mid-spring, it produces large, bell-shaped, single, bright rose-pink flowers with golden stamens. The leaves are exceptionally glossy. Height and spread 3m (10ft). 'St Ewe' makes a rounded shrub.

■ RIGHT
'GLOIRE DE NANTES'

Cultivar of *C. japonica*, introduced in 1895. From late autumn to late spring, medium-sized, usually semi-double, rich rose-pink flowers open virtually flat. Height and spread 3m (10ft). Open and upright, 'Gloire de Nantes' has one of the longest flowering seasons of any camellia.

■ ABOVE

'ELEGANS' (SYN. 'CHANDLER'S ELEGANS')

Cultivar of *C. japonica*, introduced in 1831. In mid- to late spring, it produces large, anemone-form, soft pink flowers; the central petaloids can be spotted with white. Height and spread 3m (10ft). 'Elegans' is a spreading, slow-growing shrub; it is best with minimal pruning.

■ RIGHT

'RUBESCENS MAJOR'

Cultivar of *C. japonica*, introduced in 1985. In mid-spring, it produces large, formal double or rose-form double, pinkish-crimson flowers, veined darker, among broad, rounded, light green leaves. Height and spread 2.5m (8ft). 'Rubescens Major' is a dense, compact, rounded shrub.

■ LEFT

'ANTICIPATION'

Cultivar of *C.* x *williamsii*, introduced in 1966. Very large, peony-form, deep rose-pink flowers appear freely in late winter to early spring. The leaves are glossy bright green. Height 4m (13ft), spread 2m (6½ft). Bushy, upright and slow-growing, 'Anticipation' is an ideal choice for a container or a small garden.

■ ABOVE

'ROSE PARADE'

Cultivar of *C.* x *williamsii*, introduced in 1969. Large, formal double, rich, deep rose-pink flowers are freely carried from early to late spring. Height 2.5m (8ft), spread 2m (6½ft). 'Rose Parade' grows into a dense, upright shrub.

■ ABOVE

'AKASHIGATA' (SYN. 'LADY CLARE')

Cultivar of *C. japonica*, introduced in 1887. Very large, semi-double, deep salmon-pink flowers, with yellow stamens, appear from early to late spring among broad leaves. Height 1.5m (5ft), spread 3m (10ft). The pendulous branches make 'Akashigata' suitable for training against a wall.

'LAVINIA MAGGI'
(SYN. 'CONTESSA LAVINIA MAGGI')

Cultivar of *C. japonica*, introduced in 1860. From early to mid-spring, it carries medium-sized, formal double flowers that are white to pale pink with pink and red stripes. Height and spread 2m (6½ft) or more. Bred in Italy, 'Lavinia Maggi' is one of the oldest cultivars still in general cultivation; long-flowering, it has a tendency to sport solid-coloured flowers.

■ ABOVE

'TRICOLOR' (SYN. 'SIEBOLDII')

Cultivar of *C. japonica*, introduced in 1929. In early spring, it produces medium-sized, single or semi-double flowers that have petals striped in shades of red, pink or white. The bright green leaves are crinkled. Height and spread 2m (6½ft) or more. 'Tricolor' is a dense, spreading camellia, and is one of the oldest cultivars still available.

■ ABOVE

'DR CLIFFORD PARKS'

Hybrid camellia (*C. reticulata* x *C. japonica*), introduced in 1971. Very large, semi-double, loose peony or anemone-form, deep red flowers appear in mid-spring. The leaves are oval and dark green. Height 4m (13ft), spread 2.5m (8ft). A vigorous plant, 'Dr Clifford Parks' is a rare camellia.

■ ABOVE

'JUPITER' (SYN. 'PAUL'S JUPITER')

Cultivar of *C. japonica*, introduced in 1990. From mid- to late spring, it produces medium-sized, single, bright red flowers with golden stamens; they are sometimes blotched with white. Height 3m (10ft), spread 2m (6½ft). Reliably hardy, 'Jupiter' makes a vigorous, upright shrub.

■ LEFT

'MARK ALAN'

Cultivar of *C. japonica*, introduced in 1996. Large, semi-double to loose peony-form red flowers, sometimes tinged purple, open from early to mid-spring. Height 3m (10ft), spread 2m (6½ft). 'Mark Alan' is a tall, upright and vigorous camellia.

■ ABOVE

'GRAND PRIX'

Cultivar of *C. japonica*, introduced in
1968. From mid- to late spring, it carries
very large, semi-double, brilliant clear red
flowers with yellow stamens. Height and
spread to 5m (16½ft). A vigorous, upright
shrub, 'Grand Prix' is one of the showiest
of its type; it develops a more open habit as
it matures, and is suitable for wall-training.

■ RIGHT

'APOLLO'
(SYN. 'PAUL'S APOLLO')

Cultivar of *C. japonica*, introduced in
1911. Small, semi-double red flowers, with
yellow stamens, appear from early to late
spring; they are occasionally marbled with
white. The glossy dark green leaves are
twisted at the tips. Height and spread 3m
(10ft). 'Apollo' is an open, spreading
shrub; it is exceptionally hardy and
tolerates some wind.

■ ABOVE

'BOB'S TINSIE'

Cultivar of *C. japonica*, introduced in
1962. Miniature to small, anemone-form
flowers appear in abundance from early
to late spring. The outer petals are deep
crimson; the inner petaloids are crimson
and white. The leaves are small. Height
2m (6½ft), spread 1m (3ft). A neat, twiggy,
upright plant, 'Bob's Tinsie' is a choice
and unusual cultivar.

■ RIGHT

'KRAMER'S SUPREME'

Cultivar of *C. japonica*, introduced in
1957. In late autumn and in early to
mid-spring, it produces large to very large,
scented, peony-form, bright red flowers
that open flat. Height 3m (10ft), spread
2m (6½ft). Not reliably hardy, 'Kramer's
Supreme' is best overwintered under
glass in cold areas; it makes a compact,
upright plant.

■ LEFT

'ELIZABETH HAWKINS'

Cultivar of *C. japonica*, introduced in
1973. In mid-spring, small anemone-form,
bright red flowers appear. Height and
spread 2m (6½ft). 'Elizabeth Hawkins'
makes a compact shrub.

■ RIGHT

'DR BURNSIDE'

Cultivar of *C. japonica*, introduced in 1962.
Medium-sized to large, peony-form, dark
red flowers, with yellow stamens, appear
from early to late spring. Height 3m (10ft),
spread 2m (6½ft). Upright and fairly compact,
'Dr Burnside' flowers freely.

'ADOLPHE AUDUSSON'

Cultivar of *C. japonica*, introduced in 1877. Large, semi-double, dark red flowers with white stamens appear in early to mid-spring. The leaves are glossy dark green. In warm summers, seedless fruits are produced. Height 5m (16½ft), spread 4m (13ft). An open, upright plant, raised in France, 'Adolphe Audusson' is one of the oldest and most reliable of the *japonica* cultivars.

■ RIGHT
'GRAND SLAM'

Cultivar of *C. japonica*, introduced in 1962. From mid- to late spring, large, anemone-form (sometimes semi-double), fragrant, rich dark red flowers appear. Height and spread to 5m (16½ft). 'Grand Slam' is strong and upright initially, becoming more open and spreading as it ages; the flowers are among the darkest of the reds.

■ LEFT

'BOB HOPE'

Cultivar of *C. japonica*, introduced in 1972. In mid- to late spring, it produces medium-sized to large semi-double or peony-form, rich blackish-red flowers with gold stamens. The leaves are glossy green. Height and spread 3m (10ft). A bushy plant, 'Bob Hope' is an ideal choice for a container; the flowers are the deepest red of any cultivar.

■ RIGHT

'KONRONKOKU' (SYN. 'KOURON-JURA')

Cultivar of *C. japonica*, introduced in 1930. From early to mid-spring, it produces an abundance of semi-double to formal double, deep red flowers. Height and spread 3m (10ft). Bred in Japan, 'Konronkoku' is one of the darkest red camellias.

The Grower's Guide

Buying

Camellias are available year-round at specialist nurseries and garden centres, in a range of sizes. They are usually more expensive than most other shrubs, since it is difficult to produce large saleable plants quickly (see Propagation). All camellias sold commercially are container-grown: they have spent their lives in containers and have not been grown in the open (as, for instance, deciduous trees and shrubs often are), which adds to the production costs. Price depends on the size of the plant.

Buying from a garden centre is convenient, but only the most popular varieties are likely to be available. For rarer varieties, contact specialist suppliers, many of which sell by mail order. Note that there may be a delay between ordering and despatch, since stocks of some varieties can be in short supply. If you can visit the nursery to choose your plant so much the better, as staff can offer advice on its ideal situation. They can also recommend plants for specific purposes, such as wall-training or containers.

Look for plants with well-balanced, healthy top-growth. Avoid any that have yellowing foliage or that have shed many of their leaves, as this indicates that the plant has been stressed. The top-growth should be in proportion to the roots: a large plant in a small pot will be root-bound and may fail or take a long time to establish. If possible, slide the plant from the container and check the root ball. The roots should be firm and white, and not spiralling around the pot, which indicates that the plant has spent too long in its container. Once planted, the roots would continue to grow in a spiral and the plant will be slow to establish – indeed, it may not establish at all.

■ BELOW
Camellias are available in a range of sizes. For the best selection visit a specialist supplier.

■ LEFT
Small plants are available at
supermarkets and grocery stores.

■ BELOW
'November Pink' is an unusual cultivar
that is well worth looking out for.

Many gardeners are tempted
by plants in flower. While a flowering
plant is in no way better than one not
in flower, at least you can be sure that
you are buying the plant you want.
However, most reputable nurseries
undertake to replace any plant that
has been wrongly labelled, as well as
any that fail to thrive.

Small plants that may be little
more than rooted cuttings are often
sold in outlets other than garden
centres or nurseries, such as supermarkets and grocery stores. These are
usually very cheap but may not be
named, being labelled as 'white',
'pink' or 'red', according to the
flower colour. They are best potted
on and grown on for a season or two
with some protection during winter
before being planted out in the open.

Cultivation

Camellias need acid soil. While *C. sasanqua* and its cultivars tolerate neutral or even slightly alkaline soil, they perform better in acid conditions. Soil acidity is expressed in terms of the pH scale. A pH of 5.5–6.5 is ideal for most camellias.

You should test the soil in several parts of your garden before planting, since sites that are predominantly acid can contain pockets of alkaline soil and vice versa. Use an inexpensive chemical soil-testing kit from a garden centre for a reasonably accurate result. Electronic soil-testing meters give an instant result, but are less accurate.

Camellias do best in well-drained, humus-rich soil. They do not tolerate waterlogged ground or soil that dries out completely in summer. (To improve light sandy soils and lighten heavy clay soils, see Planting.) Bearing in mind that camellias are woodland plants, choose a site sheltered from hot sun and strong winds, for example in the lee of a wall or fence, or where other shrubs or trees provide some shade and shelter. In cold latitudes with low light intensity, however, a position in full sun or very light shade may be necessary for good flower formation, which occurs during mid-summer.

CAMELLIAS THAT GROW WELL AGAINST A WALL OR FENCE
s = best in full sun
sh = tolerates full shade
w = can be wall-trained
'Akashigata' (better known as 'Lady Clare') *w*
'Apollo' *s*
'Cornish Snow' *sh*
'Dazzler' *s; w*
'Elegant Beauty' *sh; w*
'Francie L' *w*
'Grand Prix' *s; w*
'Hope'
'Hugh Evans' *s*
'J. C. Williams' *sh; w*
'Joan Trehane' *sh*
'Little Bo Peep' *s*
'Mary Phoebe Taylor'
'Snowflake' *s; w*
'Water Lily' *sh*

Feed camellias in spring and summer.

The most suitable position for most camellias is light dappled shade. Cultivars of *C. sasanqua* thrive in full sun, once established.

In cold districts, early-flowering cultivars should be planted where the morning sun will not reach them. This means that any buds frosted overnight can thaw out slowly. A shaft of direct light early in the day will thaw the frost too quickly and damage the flowers. White-flowered camellias are particularly vulnerable.

Established camellias benefit from an annual mulch of organic matter in spring to conserve soil moisture and improve soil structure as it breaks down. Apply the mulch in a doughnut-like ring around the base of the plant and keep it well away from the trunk, since contact can lead to rotting. In cold areas, protect the roots in winter with a dry mulch of straw or bracken.

Do not allow camellias to dry out in summer, since this is a crucial period when the following season's flower buds form. An annual mulch should be sufficient to keep the roots cool and moist, but during periods of prolonged drought, mist the foliage with a water spray to prevent bud drop (see Pests, diseases and other

USING A SOIL-TESTING KIT

1 Take a soil sample as directed by the instructions on the back of the kit.

2 Add water to the sample and introduce the chemical agent. Shake the container.

3 Check against the colour chart supplied. Orange indicates acid soil, green alkaline.

problems: aborted flowers). Plants grown against walls, where the soil is likely to be dry, may need supplementary summer watering.

You will also need to feed young camellias to provide for active growth in mid-spring (after flowering), and again in mid-summer for the second spell of later summer growth. Some fertilizers are specially formulated for acid-loving plants.

If there is an iron deficiency in the soil or the pH tends towards neutral, an annual dose of sequestrated iron in spring is beneficial. Apply all fertilizers in accordance with the manufacturer's instructions, and take care not to overfeed. This can result in lax, sappy growth that fails to harden before the winter, and is prone to frost damage.

Cultivation under glass

In cold areas, camellias that are not fully hardy are best grown in containers under glass over winter, then moved outside for summer. With the onset of colder weather in late autumn, bring the pots into an unheated greenhouse or conservatory. Camellias under glass will withstand drops in temperature below freezing since the air is dry and still.

If the camellias are to remain under glass all year, you will have to ensure that they do not overheat in summer. The temperature should preferably not be allowed to exceed 26°C (80°F). Keep the greenhouse or conservatory shaded and the ventilators open on hot days, and damp down the floor in the morning

and evening to raise the humidity. For feeding and watering, see Planting in containers.

EXCEPTIONALLY HARDY CAMELLIAS

'Anticipation'
'Apollo'
'Berenice Boddy'
'Bowen Bryant'
'Brigadoon'
'C. M. Hovey'
'Debbie'
'Donation'
'Inspiration'
'Jupiter'
'Leonard Messel'
'Muskoka'
'Rose Parade'
'St Ewe'

Planting

Camellias are best planted in spring, which gives them a whole season to establish before their first winter. They can, however, be planted at other times, except when the ground is frozen or during periods of drought. In cold districts, planting during the autumn and winter is not recommended. If you buy or are given a camellia during this period, keep it in a sheltered spot and protect it during harsh weather (see Planting in containers). Plant out the following spring.

Good soil preparation reduces the amount of subsequent maintenance. Dig over the site and remove any perennial weeds such as couch grass or ground elder. If the soil is very heavy and drainage is poor (sometimes indicated by a green film on the soil surface), lighten it by digging in horticultural grit at the rate of a bucketful per square metre (yard). All soils are improved by additions of organic matter, which help break up heavy soils, improving drainage, and bind light, sandy soils into larger crumbs that retain moisture. Well-rotted garden compost and leaf mould (dry leaves that have been allowed to break down over two to three years) are the best soil conditioners for camellias.

PLANTING A CAMELLIA IN GRASS

1 Mark out the planting area at least 1m (1yd) square.

2 Remove the turf within the marked area.

3 Fork over the soil and remove all grass roots and perennial weeds.

4 Dig a hole for the camellia about two or three times the width of the container.

5 For improved drainage, on heavy soils work grit into the base of the hole. Fork in leaf mould, garden compost or well-rotted farmyard manure to improve soil structure.

6 Check the planting depth. The camellia should be planted no deeper than in the pot.

7 Slide the plant from its container and tease out some of the roots with your fingers or a hand fork.

8 Set the camellia in position and backfill with the excavated soil.

9 Firm the camellia in with your hands or heel. Water the plant copiously.

Cow or horse manure should only be used if it is well rotted. Heavy applications are not recommended. Fresh unrotted manure should be avoided as should poultry manure that is high in nitrogen, as these can 'scorch' the roots.

To plant in a bed or border, dig a hole at least twice the width of the container that the camellia is in, and remove all weeds that will compete for soil moisture and nutrients. To plant in grassland, it is necessary to clear a larger site to ensure that the creeping roots of perennial grasses do not grow into the camellia's root ball.

Camellias should not be planted too deeply to avoid rotting of bark on the stem where it is in contact with the soil. The top of the root ball must be level with the surrounding soil.

Water freely during the first season after planting. In subsequent years, provided you apply a spring mulch of organic matter, supplementary watering should not be necessary except on very light sandy soil.

Keep the area around the base of the plant weed-free.

Planting in containers

Camellias thrive in containers, particularly smaller, compact cultivars. More vigorous varieties can also be successful, since their root systems are restricted and the top growth can be kept under control by regular pruning. Since camellias are heavy plants, use terracotta or stone containers to provide good ballast. Plastic pots are less stable and might blow over in strong winds.

It is customary to use ericaceous compost (soil mix) that is specially formulated for acid-loving plants. This is often based on peat which is prone to waterlogging. To improve the drainage, add horticultural grit to the compost in the ratio one part grit to two of compost. You can also replace up to half of the compost with leaf mould. A layer of grit on top of

PLANTING A CAMELLIA IN A CONTAINER

1 Place broken pots over the drainage holes at the base of the container.

2 For improved drainage, fill the container to a quarter of its depth with horticultural grit.

3 Begin to fill with ericaceous compost (soil mix), formulated for lime-hating plants.

4 Work in grit in the ratio one part grit to two parts of compost.

5 Check the compost depth. Leave a gap of about 2.5cm (1in) between the top of the root ball and the rim of the container, to allow for watering.

6 Remove the camellia plant from the container.

7 Gently tease out some of the roots with your fingers or a hand fork.

8 Set the plant in position in the middle of the container and begin to backfill with compost.

9 Top-dress with grit to keep the roots cool, and to prevent moisture from evaporating from the compost.

10 Stand the container in a sheltered spot on bricks or special pot feet, so that any excess water will drain away easily. In freezing weather, protect the roots by wrapping the container with hessian (burlap) or other insulating material.

the compost surface helps keep the roots cool in summer, and prevents excessive drying out in hot weather. Regular watering during the growing season is essential. If you live in a hard-water area, use rainwater if possible. It is particularly important to keep container-grown camellias well watered during the period when the next year's flowers are forming, generally from mid-summer to autumn. Failure to do so can result in aborted flowers. Supplementary feeding is also necessary, since the nutrient content of the compost will be depleted after six to eight weeks. Slow-release pelleted fertilizer is the easiest to apply; alternatively, use a granular fertilizer suitable for rhododendrons that will gradually release its minerals. Apply one dressing as growth starts, and another just after mid-summer. Stop feeding soon after mid-summer to allow the growth to harden before the onset of winter.

In cold districts, camellias in containers need winter protection. During periods of hard frost, either bring the plant into a light, cold place, such as a porch or unheated greenhouse, or if the container is too heavy to move, leave it *in situ* and wrap it in hessian (burlap) or some other insulating material to prevent the roots from freezing.

Given regular attention, a camellia will thrive in the same container for several years. To restrict growth, prune the camellia after flowering (see Pruning and training).

Pruning and training

In general, camellias do not need extensive pruning, and are best left alone if space allows. Otherwise, annual light pruning is necessary to maintain control. A few camellias lend themselves to formal wall-training. Young plants benefit from pruning in the early years to encourage compact, even growth. Established plants need little attention, but if it is necessary to restrict size, cut back over-vigorous shoots from the previous year's growth. Harder pruning is tolerated if necessary (see Renovation, below). Pruning is best carried out when the plant is dormant in winter, or immediately after flowering.

Some camellia cultivars are genetically unstable and have a tendency to produce stems bearing flowers of a different colour or form. Remove such growth entirely. The stems can, however, be left on the plant until summer and used for propagation, if the 'break' is significant. Plain-leaved shoots on variegated cultivars such as 'Golden Spangles' should be cut back to typical variegated growth as soon as they appear. Plain shoots are always stronger than variegated ones, since they contain more chlorophyll, the pigment that makes plants green; if left untreated, the whole plant will eventually revert to plain green.

Pruning always stimulates vigorous new growth from the point where the cut is made. Therefore, make the cut just above a bud lying in the direction you wish the new shoot to grow.

Make sure your tools are clean and sharp. Rusty or dirty tools may snag the wood, creating an entry point for disease. Secateurs (pruners) are suitable for most camellia pruning, but on older plants a pruning saw may be needed. Clean your tool blades with an oily rag after use.

Pruning young plants

Young plants are sometimes leggy or lopsided, particularly if they have

PRUNING YOUNG PLANTS

1 Use secateurs (pruners) to cut out any weak, spindly growth entirely.

2 Shorten overlong stems by about one-third to a half.

3 Remove crossing stems.

■ BELOW
Camellias usually respond well to hard pruning. The dead stump should be cut back further.

■ BELOW
Most modern cultivars are 'self-grooming', and shed their flowers naturally as they fade.

■ BELOW
Some older cultivars of *C. japonica* hold on to their dead flowers. Twist them off as they fade.

been grown close together in the nursery. They will need pruning to promote bushiness. Cut out any weak or dead growth entirely, and shorten lax branches by one-third to a half or more if they are excessively leggy.

Deadheading

Most cultivars of *C. x williamsii* and many of the more recent varieties of *C. japonica* shed their flowers naturally as they fade, and do not require deadheading. The flowers of some older *C. japonica* cultivars,

however, persist and need removing, since they are unsightly. Twist them off just above a growth bud as they begin to fade.

Renovation

Old, neglected plants that have either grown out of shape or have outgrown their allotted space can be renovated by hard pruning. Cut back all the top-growth to leave a framework of old stems like an old-fashioned hat rack or, more drastically, down to 25–30cm (9–12in). This is best done in early

spring, just as the new growth begins to emerge. Camellias usually respond well to this treatment, producing new buds from the bare wood in late summer, but if you are nervous about such drastic action cut back only one-third initially. The following year, assuming the pruned stems have made a good recovery, cut back a second third, and the remaining stems the following season. Recovery can be slow, however, and it will be two to three years before the plant begins to flower freely again, but the camellia will be bushy and manageable once more.

TRAINING A CAMELLIA AGAINST A WALL

1 Dig a hole at least 30cm (1ft) from the wall.

2 Set the plant in position. Angle the top-growth towards the wall and the roots away from it.

3 Hammer in vine eyes, approximately 1m (3ft) apart. On wooden fences or brick, the screw-in type can be used.

Wall-training

Cultivars with lax stems can be formally trained against a wall or fence to produce a block of flowers. Bear in mind, however, that walls cast a rain shadow: the soil at the foot of the wall does not receive as much rainfall as soil in the open garden. Plants for wall-training should therefore be planted at least 30cm (1ft) away from the wall, with their roots angled towards the open ground. However, it will still be necessary to water the plant during periods of drought, even when established (see Cultivation).

Train in strong new shoots as they appear, building up a framework in horizontal tiers. Cut out entirely any

4 Run lengths of horticultural twine or wire between the eyes. Spread out the stems horizontally, and tie them to the twine or wire with short lengths of twine or wire. Train further stems horizontally as they grow.

shoots growing towards the wall, and any that are badly placed or cannot be trained.

Pruning hedges

Trim hedges lightly after flowering, to promote compact, even growth. It is not desirable to achieve the same dense, even surface as is found on some other evergreen non-flowering hedges, such as yew or box, however, as the flowers need space to expand. Long, vigorous shoots, which tend to grow out late in the growing season, may be cut back to keep the hedge tidy. Flower buds should already have formed on earlier growth, which should be left undisturbed.

Propagation

■ BELOW
Hybrid camellias are easily
increased by cuttings.

Camellias are usually propagated by cuttings taken in late summer or autumn from the current season's growth. Such growth is described as 'semi-ripe': it is just beginning to harden and become woody at the base, but the shoot tip is still relatively pliable. Cuttings can also be taken later, up to the end of winter, but will take longer to root. Some cultivars are slower to root than others.

Warmth and humidity are required for success. For the amateur, mist propagators are available but expensive. Small heated propagators usually generate sufficient humidity for rooting to occur, but accommodate a limited number of cuttings.

When preparing the cuttings, use a sharp knife that will make clean cuts. Dip the blade into a fungicidal solution after each cut. Wounding the base of each cutting usually encourages rooting. Good hygiene is essential, since the conditions necessary for rooting are also favourable to bacteria and fungi.

You can take the cuttings as stem-tip cuttings, as is usual for most other shrubs. However, lower portions of the stem (stem cuttings) can also be used. Owing to the expense involved in rooting the cuttings, commercial growers (and some amateurs) generally prefer to cut the stem into even shorter sections (leaf bud cuttings) to produce the maximum number of new plants from the available material. Some enthusiasts propagate by grafting, particularly to increase stocks of some *reticulata* hybrids that do not always form roots readily from cuttings. Choose strong, healthy growth that is characteristic of the plant for propagation.

Taking the cuttings

Cut lengths of the current season's growth from the plant. Cut just above a leaf bud that is pointing in the direction you wish the stem to grow the following year.

PROPAGATING BY SEMI-RIPE STEM-TIP CUTTINGS

1 Cut a length of the current season's growth. Trim each cutting just below the second or third leaf beneath the terminal leaves at the stem tip.

2 Cut off the lowest one or two leaves from the base of each cutting.

3 Remove a sliver of bark about 1–2.5cm (½–1in) long from the base of each cutting, opposite the lowest leaf bud.

For tip cuttings, trim the stem just below the second or third leaf below the pair of terminal leaves at the shoot tip. Cut off the bottom one or two leaves. Opposite the lowest leaf, cut away a sliver of bark about 1–2.5cm (½–1in) long.

For stem cuttings, cut the stem into lengths, each piece with three leaves. Trim each cutting just above the uppermost leaf and just below the lowest. Cut off the lowest leaf, then remove a sliver of bark on the opposite side of the stem as for tip cuttings, above.

For leaf bud cuttings, cut the stem just above each leaf. Cut off a sliver of bark about 5mm (¼in) long at the base on the opposite side of the leaf.

Rooting the cuttings

Prepare a cuttings compost (rooting medium) of one part peat (or an alternative) to one of grit (or perlite or vermiculite). Fill 7cm (3in) pots or trays with the compost and moisten it either by misting with a spray or by standing the containers in a bowl of shallow water and allowing the compost to become wet by capillary action. Drain the container. Treat the base of each cutting with hormone rooting compound, following the manufacturer's instructions.

Next, insert the cuttings in the compost using a dibber. The lowest leaf should be just above, not in contact with, the compost surface.

Firm the cuttings in gently, and mist with a fungicidal solution. Label the cuttings and place them in a closed heated propagator. Alternatively, tent the container in a clear plastic bag supported on canes and place it over a heat source such as a soil-warming cable. Keep cuttings partially shaded.

Camellia cuttings should root in nine to twelve weeks. To check whether they have rooted, give each cutting a gentle tug. If you feel resistance, the cutting has rooted. If the cutting has not rooted but still looks healthy, refirm the compost and leave undisturbed for at least another three to four weeks. Too much checking inhibits rooting.

4 Dip the base of each cutting into hormone rooting compound.

5 Insert the cuttings into pots of peat (or an alternative) and grit, perlite or vermiculite.

6 Mist with a fungicide to kill bacteria and fungal spores.

Aftercare

Once the cuttings have rooted, gradually open the vents of the propagator lid or remove the plastic bag for short intervals over a period of about a week to acclimatize the cuttings to less humid air. After two to three weeks, remove the coverings entirely.

Keep the cuttings under glass during the first winter. In late winter to early spring, pot them up individually into 7cm (3in) pots of ericaceous compost (soil mix). (Pot up cuttings taken in autumn or winter in late spring or early summer.) Grow them on in a cold frame or under glass and feed and water them regularly (see Planting in

containers). Pot them on the following spring and gradually acclimatize them to outdoor conditions, standing them outside during the day but protecting them against night frosts. Keep them under cover for the second winter, and continue growing them on in containers for a second season as described.

In areas with mild winters, they should be large enough to plant out in the autumn; in cooler areas, overwinter them under glass and plant them out the following spring when all danger of frost has passed.

7 Label the cuttings, and tent them in a clear plastic bag supported on canes.

Pests, diseases and other problems

Camellias grown outdoors in situations that suit them are generally free of pests and diseases, or are easily treated if they fall prey to any attack. Some pests, such as aphids, can be more problematic under glass, while plants in containers are susceptible to vine weevils. To help keep pot plants overwintered under glass pest-free, move them outside in spring, where the pests' natural predators will be present in greater numbers.

When using any proprietary insecticide or fungicide, always follow the manufacturer's instructions. Dilute the product as directed and apply at the recommended rate. Wear protective clothing as recommended, and wash your hands carefully after handling any chemicals.

The following are some of the problems you are most likely to encounter.

Aborted flowers

How to identify: Flower buds develop but fail to open or drop from the plant.
Cause: Any number of cultivation problems, the likeliest being lack of water during the period of bud formation the previous

Aborted flower

summer. A sudden cold spell in spring can also lead to aborted flowers.
Control: None possible.
Prevention: Make sure the plant does not dry out during late summer when next year's flower buds are forming.

Aphids and scale insects

How to identify: Aphids, which suck sap, are seen on the young leaves at the start of the growing season. Failure to deal with them can result in sooty mould. Scale insects are found on the undersides of older leaves. The most common are very small and pale brown. The white woolly egg cases seen in early

summer are more visible.
Cause: Aphids and scale insects are virtually endemic in gardens; they are more likely to pose problems under glass, however, where conditions favour them and their predators may not be present.
Control: Spray with a

Aphids

systemic insecticide, such as malathion or permethrin, in late spring, early summer and autumn, paying particular attention to the undersides of the leaves. Under glass, vaporizing strips can be used. On small plants, the pest can be removed by hand.
Prevention: Spraying in spring, before the pest appears, can be effective, but repeated sprayings later may be necessary.

Honey fungus

How to identify: Growth is poor and plants look yellow and sick; in severe cases, the camellia dies.
Cause: Honey fungus (*Armillaria mellea*) appears as honey-coloured toadstools that are visible on old tree stumps in the autumn; below ground, long, shoelace-like growths spread out and destroy the roots of neighbouring plants.
Control: No known control is fully effective, but removal of old tree stumps and roots before planting reduces the risk. It is possible to revive an infected plant by a fungicide drench (Armillatox), followed by a high nitrogen feed to encourage growth in spring.
Prevention: Do not plant camellias near old tree stumps that may attract the fungus.

Leaf mottle virus

How to identify: Leaves are mottled with yellow; flowers can be blotched with white. The disease is endemic in some older varieties.
Cause: A mosaic virus. The infection can be spread from plant to plant during propagation if the tools are not kept scrupulously clean.
Control: None possible. The virus does no long-term harm to the plant, but can affect flower quality.
Prevention: Practise good hygiene when propagating. Buy only virus-free stock.

Petal blight

How to identify: Blooms are patched with brown or fail to open.
Cause: The fungus *Ciborinia camelliae* most prevalent in humid conditions. The disease originated in Japan, spread to the USA and New Zealand and has been detected in Portugal, Spain and parts of France.
Control: None yet available. Research is concentrated on biological control.
Prevention: Remove and destroy all dead flowers from around the base of the plant. Buy only guaranteed disease-free stock.

Sooty mould

How to identify: Leaves are covered with a blackish fungus.
Cause: Failure to eradicate aphids and scale insects.

Sooty mould

Their excretion (honeydew) forms a base for the mould.
Control: Remove the mould with a damp sponge or cloth, then spray with a fungicide.
Prevention: Control aphids and scale insects (see above).

Sporting

How to identify: Flowers of a different colour or form are spontaneously produced.
Cause: Not identifiable, but possibly caused by some check to the plant, such as a sudden cold spell. Some cultivars, particularly those with bicoloured flowers, are more likely to sport than others.

Control: None possible. Sporting is evidence of unstable genes.
Prevention: Not possible. Any uncharacteristic growth should be removed, but can be used for propagation purposes if it represents a novelty. Sporting can be a positive feature, since many new varieties arise as sports.

Vine weevils

How to identify: Adult vine weevils are dark brown with white speckles on their bodies. They eat notches from the edges of leaves, and although this is unsightly it does no damage of any consequence to the plant. Worse damage is caused by the creamy white larvae that are seldom seen and attack the roots of plants in late spring and summer.
Cause: Failure to eradicate the parent before it lays its eggs in spring and summer.

Vine weevil

Control: To control larvae, use an insecticidal root drench. Older larvae are resistant to the chemical controls available; to control them, introduce parasitic nematodes into the compost in late summer.
Prevention: Maintain good hygiene. Adult beetles usually hide under pots or pot rims. Examine the soil of any bought-in smaller plants, especially *Cyclamen,* for grubs which tend to be deep in the root ball in loose soil.

Wild animals

How to identify: In rural areas, rabbits, hares and deer gnaw at the bark of young plants, in many cases causing the death of the plant.
Cause: Wild animals are most likely to pose a problem in gardens that adjoin open fields or woodland.
Control: Protect the trunks of young plants with tree-guard collars, or surround them with wire mesh stapled to stout stakes.
Prevention: Erect a fence around the garden, sunk at least 45cm (18in) into the ground to deter burrowing mammals. A height of 1m (3ft) is sufficient to keep out rabbits and hares; allow 2m (6½ft) for deer.

Calendar

■ BELOW
In cold districts, protect tender camellias under glass with horticultural fleece.

Spring

Plant new stock; prune if necessary. Cut back any stems that have sported. Deadhead any varieties that do not shed their flowers naturally. Feed and mulch established plants. Treat established plants with sequestrated iron, if necessary. Top-dress camellias in containers. Prune after flowering, if necessary. Hard prune any old, neglected plants. Watch for, and treat, aphid infestations. Move plants grown under glass into the open, once all danger of hard frost has passed. Move cuttings taken the previous year into a cold frame outdoors.

Summer

Keep newly planted camellias well watered, especially during dry spells. Water camellias in containers freely. Continue to control aphid infestations. Apply an insecticidal root drench to plants in containers attacked by vine weevils. During prolonged periods of drought, mist over established plants under glass or in dry situations in the garden and water any plants grown against walls or fences thoroughly in the evening. Continue to plant new stock during suitable weather. Take cuttings to increase your stock from late summer onwards.

Autumn

Plant new stock (in mild areas only). Take cuttings. In cold districts, bring tender camellias that have spent the summer outdoors back under glass before the first hard frost.

Winter

Protect plants grown in containers, either by wrapping them in hessian (burlap) or another insulating material, or by moving them under cover. Cover the roots of established plants with a dry mulch such as bracken or straw to protect them over winter. Prune to restrict growth or to renovate neglected plants.

Water camellias with a solution of sequestrated iron in spring, if necessary.

Other recommended camellias

Besides the camellias described in the Plant Directory, the following are recommended. Heights and spreads, not specified here, can vary depending on the local climate, and can be restricted by careful pruning. Flowering times vary from year to year, depending on the weather.

'**Ada Pieper**' Cultivar of *C. japonica* with large, peony-form, coral-pink flowers in early to late spring. Slow-growing.

'**Alexander Hunter**' Cultivar of *C. japonica* with medium-sized, single or semi-double deep crimson flowers in early and mid-spring. Upright.

'**Anemone Frill**' Cultivar of *C. x williamsii* with anemone- or peony-form, mid-pink flowers in mid- to late spring. Upright and slightly open.

'**Ann Sothern**' Cultivar of *C. japonica* with large, semi-double, pale pink flowers in early to mid-spring. Vigorous, upright and compact.

'**Annie Wylam**' Cultivar of *C. japonica* with peony-form, pink flowers in early to late spring. Open and upright.

'**Betty Foy Sanders**' Cultivar of *C. japonica* with flared, trumpet-shaped white flowers, streaked with red, from early to mid-spring. Bushy and upright.

'**Black Lace**' Cultivar of *C. x williamsii* with formal double, deep red flowers in mid- to late spring. Slow and upright.

'Alexander Hunter'

'**Blaze of Glory**' Cultivar of *C. japonica* with peony-form, bright red flowers in early spring among large, dark green leaves. Upright and open.

'**Bokuhan**' Cultivar of *C. japonica* with anemone-form flowers; the outer petals are bright red, surrounding dense, white centres. Vigorous and upright.

'**Bow Bells**' Cultivar of *C. x williamsii* with an abundance of bell-shaped, mid-pink flowers in early to late spring. Upright.

'**Bowen Bryant**' Cultivar of *C. x williamsii* with large, bowl-shaped, semi-double, pink flowers from mid- to late spring. Upright.

'**Bridal Gown**' Cultivar of *C. x williamsii* with peony-form white flowers in mid- to late spring, among light green leaves. Compact and upright.

'**Captain Rawes**' Cultivar of *C. reticulata* with very large, semi-double, carmine-red flowers in late spring. Spreading and tree-like.

'**Carter's Sunburst**' Cultivar of *C. japonica* with peony-form or double, pale pink flowers, striped deeper pink, in mid-spring. Compact and upright shrub.

'**Charles Colbert**' Cultivar of *C. x williamsii* with large, semi-double, light pink flowers in mid- to late spring. Prolific.

'**Charles Michael**' Cultivar of *C. x williamsii* with large, single, trumpet-shaped, pale pink flowers in mid- to late spring. Broad and fairly bushy.

'Debutante'

'**Charlotte de Rothschild**' Cultivar of *C. japonica* with single white flowers with pale gold stamens in mid-spring. Slow, upright and slightly open shrub.

'**Cheryl Lynn**' Cultivar of *C. japonica* with large, formal double, light pink flowers in mid-spring. Upright and open.

'Desire'

'**Clarise Carlton**' Cultivar of *C. japonica* with loose, semi-double, light red flowers from early to late spring. Upright and open.

'**Commander Mulroy**' Cultivar of *C. japonica* with formal double, pure white flowers that open from pink buds in mid-spring. Dense and upright.

'**Cornish Spring**' Hybrid camellia with small, single pink flowers from mid- to late spring. Open and twiggy as a young plant, compact and bushy when mature; needs good light for free flowering.

'**Daintiness**' Cultivar of *C. x williamsii* with an abundance of long-lasting, semi-double, salmon-pink flowers in mid-spring. Makes a dainty shrub.

'Dazzler' Cultivar of
C. sasanqua with semi-double
or loose peony-form, brilliant
pinkish-red flowers from
mid- to late autumn. Good
for wall-training.

'E. G. Waterhouse'

'Debutante' Cultivar of
C. japonica with peony-form,
pale pink flowers in mid-
spring. Upright and compact.
'Desire' Cultivar of
C. japonica with formal
double flowers; the petals
are white, edged deeper
pink at the points. Strong
and upright.
'Donnan's Dream' Cultivar
of *C. japonica* with medium-
sized to large, formal double,
white flowers, shaded with
orchid pink, in early to late
spring. Compact and upright.
'Dream Boat' Cultivar of
C. x *williamsii* with large,
formal double, bright pink
flowers in mid-spring.
Upright and bushy.

'E. G. Waterhouse' Cultivar
of *C.* x *williamsii* with formal
double, light pink flowers
from mid- to late spring.
Narrow and upright.
'El Dorado' Cultivar of
C. x *williamsii* with large,
peony-form, light pink
flowers in mid-spring.
Free-flowering.
'Elegans Champagne'
Cultivar of *C. japonica* with
anemone-form, white flowers,
with cream centres, in mid-
to late spring. Best under glass
in cold districts.
'Elegant Beauty' Cultivar of
C. x *williamsii* with masses
of anemone-form, deep pink
flowers on arching stems in
late spring; the young leaves
are tinged bronze. Suitable for
wall-training.

'Elegans Champagne'

'Elizabeth Anderson' Cultivar
of *C.* x *williamsii* with formal
double, pink flowers among
light green leaves in mid-
spring. Upright.

'Elsie Jury' Cultivar of
C. x *williamsii* with large,
peony-form, clear pale pink
flowers from mid- to late
spring. Open and upright.
'Extravaganza' Cultivar of
C. japonica with large, peony-
form flowers in mid-spring
that are white, striped and
patched with red. Compact
and upright.
'Felice Harris' Cultivar of
C. x *williamsii* with semi-
double, pale ivory-pink
flowers in mid- to late spring.
An upright shrub.
'Firedance' Cultivar of
C. japonica with semi-double,
tubular, deep red flowers in
mid-spring. Compact.
'Flower Girl' A hybrid
camellia with semi-double
to peony-form, lightly
scented, pink flowers in
early spring. Upright.
'Fragrant Pink' Hybrid
camellia with small, peony-
form, scented, deep pink
flowers in early to mid-
spring. Open and upright;
needs a warm site.
'Francie L' Hybrid camellia
with large, semi-double,
salmon-red flowers in mid-
spring. Strong and upright;
can be wall-trained.
'Francis Hanger' Cultivar of
C. x *williamsii* with masses
of single white flowers with
yellow stamens from mid-
to late spring. Makes slow,
spreading growth.

'Freedom Bell' Cultivar of
C. x *williamsii* with small, bell-
shaped, semi-double bright red
flowers in mid- to late spring.
Compact and upright.

'Little Bit'

'Galaxie' Cultivar of
C. x *williamsii* with double
to rose-form, pink flowers,
striped darker pink, from
early to late spring.
Moderately vigorous.
'Garden Glory' Cultivar of
C. x *williamsii* with formal
double, rich pink flowers
in early to late spring. Slow
growing and compact as
it matures.
'George Blandford' Cultivar
of *C.* x *williamsii* with peony-
form, bright crimson-pink
flowers from early to late
spring. A rounded shrub.
'Hagoromo' (syn. 'Magnolii-
flora') Cultivar of *C. japonica*
with semi-double white
flowers, flushed pink, in mid-
spring. Compact and upright.

'Hakurakuten' Cultivar of
C. japonica with large, peony-form white flowers in early spring. Vigorous and upright.

'Hanatachibana' Cultivar of *C. japonica* with formal double, coral-pink flowers from mid- to late spring. Compact and upright.

'Hawaii' Cultivar of *C. japonica* with large, peony-form, pale pink flowers in mid- to late spring. Slow and upright.

'Hope' Cultivar of *C. x williamsii* with peony-form, very pale pink flowers among light green leaves in mid- to late spring. Vigorous.

'Hugh Evans' Cultivar of *C. sasanqua* with masses of single pink flowers in mid-autumn. Upright and bushy.

'Jill Totty' Cultivar of *C. x williamsii* with large, peony-form, pure white flowers in mid- to late spring. Bushy.

'Joyful Bells' Cultivar of *C. x williamsii* with small, single, wine-red flowers in mid-spring. Vigorous; best in a sheltered spot.

'Jury's Charity' Cultivar of *C. x williamsii* with large, semi-double, rich rose-pink flowers in mid- to late spring. Bushy and prolific.

'Just Darling' Cultivar of *C. japonica* with miniature, formal double, pale pink flowers in mid- to late spring. Upright and vigorous.

'Kewpie Doll' Cultivar of *C. japonica* with miniature, anemone-form, pale pink flowers, marked deeper pink, in mid-spring. Bushy and upright.

'Lovelight'

'Kick Off' Cultivar of *C. japonica* with large, peony-form, pale pink flowers, marked deeper pink, from early to mid-spring. Vigorous and upright.

'Kitty Berry' Cultivar of *C. japonica* with loose peony-form, peach pink flowers in early spring. Strong, dense and upright.

'Lady Vansittart' Cultivar of *C. japonica* with semi-double, white flowers, striped pink to red, from early to mid-spring. Upright and compact. It sports freely to plain red or plain white.

'Laura Boscawen' Cultivar of *C. x williamsii* with an abundance of anemone-form, coral-pink flowers from mid- to late spring. Has dark green leaves. Compact and upright.

'Lemon Drop' Cultivar of *C. japonica* with rose-form, white flowers with lemon-yellow centres in mid-spring. Dense and upright.

'Lily Pons' Cultivar of *C. japonica* with large, single to semi-double white flowers in mid- to late spring; the long, narrow petals surround a barrel-like boss of golden stamens. Upright and fairly open shrub.

'Little Bit' Cultivar of *C. japonica* with anemone-form flowers in mid-spring that can be white flecked with red or solid red. Makes an upright, rounded bush.

'Little Bo Peep' Cultivar of *C. japonica* with miniature, formal double, pale pink flowers in mid-spring. Vigorous and upright.

'Mary Phoebe Taylor'

'Lovelight' Cultivar of *C. japonica* with large, semi-double white flowers in mid-spring. Leaves are large and glossy. Vigorous and spreading.

'Margaret Davis Picotee' Cultivar of *C. japonica* with formal double to loose peony-form white flowers in spring; petals have red borders. Upright and vigorous.

'Mariann' Cultivar of *C. japonica* with medium-sized to large, anemone-form, lightly scented, red flowers in early to late spring. Vigorous and upright.

'Mona Jury'

'Mary Costa' Cultivar of *C. japonica* with large, anemone-form, white flowers in mid-spring. Upright and fairly compact.

'Mary Phoebe Taylor' Cultivar of *C. x williamsii* with large, loose peony-form or semi-double, pale pink flowers in mid- to late spring. Vigorous, upright and spreading.

'Masayoshi' (syn. 'Donckelaeri') Cultivar of *C. japonica* with irregularly double white flowers, marbled with red, from mid- to late spring. Vigorous.

'Mathotiana Alba' Cultivar of *C. japonica* with rose-form double white flowers in mid- to late spring. Vigorous.

'Matterhorn' Cultivar of *C. japonica* with formal double, white flowers in mid- to late spring. Upright and fairly compact.

'Patricia Ann'

'Mattie Cole' Cultivar of *C. japonica* with large, single, salmon-pink flowers in early to mid-spring. Free-flowering.

'Midnight Serenade' Cultivar of *C. japonica* with single, funnel-shaped, deep red flowers among dark green leaves in mid- to late spring. Upright and open.

'Mirage' Cultivar of *C. x williamsii* with masses of semi-double, cerise-pink flowers in early to late spring. Upright and slightly open.

'Miss Universe' Cultivar of *C. japonica* with formal double, white flowers in late spring. Stiff and spreading; a reliable white in cold areas.

'Mona Jury' Cultivar of *C. x williamsii* with loose peony-form, warm pink flowers in mid- to late spring. Open and spreading.

'Mrs D. W. Davis' Cultivar of *C. japonica* with semi-double, light pink flowers from late winter to mid-spring. Vigorous and upright.

'Narumigata' Cultivar of *C. sasanqua* with small, cupped, single, fragrant white flowers, edged with pink, in autumn. Upright and good against a wall.

'November Pink' Cultivar of *C. x williamsii* with an abundance of single pink flowers from mid-winter to late spring, and occasionally in early winter. Prune regularly to keep compact.

'Scentuous'

'Nuccio's Cameo' Cultivar of *C. japonica* with medium-sized to large, formal double (occasionally rose-form), coral-pink flowers in early to late spring. Upright, bushy and compact.

'Nuccio's Gem' Cultivar of *C. japonica* with formal double, white flowers in mid-spring; the petals are arranged in spirals. Compact and upright.

'Seagull'

C. oleifera Species from China with medium-sized single, fragrant white flowers, occasionally tipped with pink, from late autumn. Often confused with 'Narumigata' which it closely resembles.

'Patricia Ann' Cultivar of *C. japonica* with very large, semi-double, pale pink flowers from mid- to late spring; the petals are washed with creamy white at the centre. Upright.

'Perfecta' Cultivar of *C. x williamsii* with formal double, rose-pink flowers in mid- to late spring. Dense and free-flowering.

'Primavera' Cultivar of *C. japonica* with formal double, white flowers in mid- to late spring that weather well. Upright and bushy.

'R. L. Wheeler' Cultivar of *C. japonica* with very large, anemone- or peony-form rose-pink flowers in mid-spring. Spreading; susceptible to leaf mottle virus.

'Royalty' Cultivar of *C. reticulata* with very large, semi-double, light red flowers in mid-spring; the petals are crinkled and wavy. Upright and spreading.

'Ruddigore' Cultivar of *C. japonica* with masses of large, loose peony-form, light red flowers in mid- to late spring. Upright and compact.

'San Dimas' Cultivar of *C. japonica* with semi-double, rich dark red flowers with yellow stamens; the leaves are dark green. A compact and bushy shrub.

'Satan's Robe' Hybrid camellia with large, semi-double carmine-red flowers in spring. Vigorous and upright shrub.

'Sayonara' Cultivar of *C. x williamsii* with semi-double, cup-shaped, clear pink flowers in early to late spring. Upright and vigorous.

'Scentuous' Hybrid camellia with miniature to small, fragrant, loose peony-form flowers in mid-spring; the petals are white, flushed pink at the edges. Best under glass in cold districts.

'Seagull' Cultivar of
C. japonica with large,
semi-double or loose peony-
form, white flowers in
mid-spring; the wavy petals
surround yellow stamens.
Vigorous and spreading.
'Señorita' Cultivar of
C. x williamsii with masses
of peony-form, pink flowers
in mid- to late spring; the
petals are wavy. Bushy and
upright shrub.

'Tinker Toy'

'Shiro Wabisuke' Cultivar
of *C. japonica* with single,
fragrant, white flowers over
a long period in early spring.
Very hardy.
'Show Girl' Camellia
hybrid with large, semi-
double, clear pink flowers
in early to mid-spring.
Vigorous, open and upright.
C. sinensis Known as the
tea plant. Species from
northern India, Burma,
Thailand and China with
very small single, waxy
white flowers from late
autumn to mid-winter.

Best cultivated under glass
in cold areas.
'Snowflake' Cultivar of
C. sasanqua with single white
flowers in autumn to winter.
Good for wall-training.
'Spring Festival' Hybrid
camellia with double pink
flowers in mid- to late
spring; the leaves are
tinged bronze when young.
Narrow and upright; best
in a sunny site.
'Spring Mist' Hybrid
with small, semi-double,
scented, blush pink to
white flowers in mid-spring.
Needs a sheltered site.
'Tinker Toy' Cultivar of
C. japonica with miniature,
anemone-form white flowers
from mid- to late spring that
are speckled and striped red;
the leaves are light green.
Compact and upright.

'Tom Thumb'

'Tiptoe' Cultivar of
C. x williamsii with semi-
double, pale pink flowers in
mid- to late spring. Bushy and

slow-growing; use in a
container or as a hedge.
'Tom Knudsen' Cultivar
of *C. japonica* with peony-
form, dark red flowers from
early to mid-spring. Sturdy
and upright.
'Tom Thumb' Cultivar of
C. japonica with small, formal
double flowers from mid-
to late spring; the petals are
pink, edged white. Bushy.
'Tomorrow' Cultivar of
C. japonica with peony-
form, light red flowers from
mid- to late spring. Vigorous
and spreading.
'Vittorio Emanuele II'
Cultivar of *C. japonica* with
formal double, deep pink
flowers, streaked with red
and with white petaloids,
in mid-spring. Open and
upright.
'Water Lily' Cultivar of
C. x williamsii with formal
double, pink flowers in
mid-spring; the petals curve
inwards, hence the name.
Best pruned when young
to develop a bushy habit.
'Wilamina' Cultivar of
C. japonica with small, formal
double, pink flowers, edged
with white, in mid-spring.
Slow-growing.
'Wilber Foss' Cultivar of
C. x williamsii with large,
peony-form, brilliant pinkish-
red flowers from mid- to late
spring. Compact, moderately
vigorous and upright.

'William Bartlett' Cultivar
of *C. japonica* with formal
double, pale pink flowers,
striped and flecked with
deeper pink, in mid- to late
spring. Bushy, compact
and upright.
'William Honey' Cultivar
of *C. japonica* with peony-
form white flowers, flecked
and striped crimson,
from mid- to late spring.
Bushy; the branches are
slightly pendulous.

'Yuletide'

'Yours Truly' Cultivar of
C. japonica with semi-
double, pink flowers,
veined and bordered
with white, in late spring.
Upright and vigorous.
'Yuletide' Cultivar of
C. sasanqua with small,
single, bright red flowers with
bright yellow stamens in late
autumn to winter. Compact
and upright. Best under glass
in cold districts.

Index

ACKNOWLEDGEMENTS
The publisher would like to thank the following people for allowing photography of their gardens: Trehane Camellia Nursery, Dorset; Ann Hartley, Long Buckby, Northants; and Chris Margrave at Wentworth Castle, South Yorkshire. We would also like to thank the following people for allowing reproduction of their photographs: John Glover at The Garden Picture Library, 6–7; The Harry Smith Collection, 12, 43r, 59b, 63r; Jennifer Trehane, 19tl and tr, 60l; and Peter McHoy, 57b.